# Password Passport

## By Linda Fostek

This book is dedicated to everyone who has hit the Password Reset Button one too many times.

Anyone who has been frustrated by the ever more complicated password instructions aimed at protecting us from those who wish to do us harm.

Instructions that make us feel stupid and seem to end up protecting us only from ourselves, resulting in another round of "Password Reset" the next time we want to access our account.

For all those, who have a password frame of sticky notes around our computer but, never seem to be able to find the one we need.

And for those, who routinely change their passwords just to prevent the possibility of being hacked and would like to have a record of passwords you have already used.

Introducing a simple, low tech solution that provides an easy to update format putting all those pesky passwords in their place.

Welcome to your Password Passport

# Password Essentials

| Device | Password |
|---|---|
| Home Computer | |
| Home Computer | |
| Work Computer | |
| Cell Phone | |
| Cell Phone | |
| Tablet | |
| Tablet | |
| | |
| | |
| | |

# Special Notes and Instructions for my family:

# A

| Company/Product | URL | Log-in |
| --- | --- | --- |
| | | |
| **Password** | | |
| **& Revised** | | |
| **Passwords** | | |
| Company/Product | URL | Log-in |
| | | |
| **Password** | | |
| **& Revised** | | |
| **Passwords** | | |
| Company/Product | URL | Log-in |
| | | |
| **Password** | | |
| **& Revised** | | |
| **Passwords** | | |
| Company/Product | URL | Log-in |
| | | |
| **Password** | | |
| **& Revised** | | |
| **Passwords** | | |

| Company/Product | URL | Log-in |
| --- | --- | --- |
|  |  |  |

| Password | | | |
| --- | --- | --- | --- |
| & Revised | | | |
| Passwords | | | |

| Company/Product | URL | Log-in |
| --- | --- | --- |
|  |  |  |

| Password | | | |
| --- | --- | --- | --- |
| & Revised | | | |
| Passwords | | | |

| Company/Product | URL | Log-in |
| --- | --- | --- |
|  |  |  |

| Password | | | |
| --- | --- | --- | --- |
| & Revised | | | |
| Passwords | | | |

| Company/Product | URL | Log-in |
| --- | --- | --- |
|  |  |  |

| Password | | | |
| --- | --- | --- | --- |
| & Revised | | | |
| Passwords | | | |

| Company/Product | URL | Log-in |
| --- | --- | --- |
|  |  |  |
| Password |  |  |  |
| & Revised |  |  |  |
| Passwords |  |  |  |
| Company/Product | URL | Log-in |
|  |  |  |
| Password |  |  |  |
| & Revised |  |  |  |
| Passwords |  |  |  |
| Company/Product | URL | Log-in |
|  |  |  |
| Password |  |  |  |
| & Revised |  |  |  |
| Passwords |  |  |  |
| Company/Product | URL | Log-in |
|  |  |  |
| Password |  |  |  |
| & Revised |  |  |  |
| Passwords |  |  |  |

| Company/Product | URL | Log-in |
| --- | --- | --- |
|  |  |  |
| Password | | |
| & Revised | | |
| Passwords | | |
| Company/Product | URL | Log-in |
|  |  |  |
| Password | | |
| & Revised | | |
| Passwords | | |
| Company/Product | URL | Log-in |
|  |  |  |
| Password | | |
| & Revised | | |
| Passwords | | |
| Company/Product | URL | Log-in |
|  |  |  |
| Password | | |
| & Revised | | |
| Passwords | | |

# B

| Company/Product | URL | Log-in |
| --- | --- | --- |
|  |  |  |
| Password |  |  |  |
| & Revised |  |  |  |
| Passwords |  |  |  |
| Company/Product | URL | Log-in |
|  |  |  |
| Password |  |  |  |
| & Revised |  |  |  |
| Passwords |  |  |  |
| Company/Product | URL | Log-in |
|  |  |  |
| Password |  |  |  |
| & Revised |  |  |  |
| Passwords |  |  |  |
| Company/Product | URL | Log-in |
|  |  |  |
| Password |  |  |  |
| & Revised |  |  |  |
| Passwords |  |  |  |

| Company/Product | | URL | Log-in |
|---|---|---|---|
| | | | |
| Password | | | |
| & Revised | | | |
| Passwords | | | |
| Company/Product | | URL | Log-in |
| | | | |
| Password | | | |
| & Revised | | | |
| Passwords | | | |
| Company/Product | | URL | Log-in |
| | | | |
| Password | | | |
| & Revised | | | |
| Passwords | | | |
| Company/Product | | URL | Log-in |
| | | | |
| Password | | | |
| & Revised | | | |
| Passwords | | | |

| Company/Product | URL | Log-in |
| --- | --- | --- |
| | | |
| Password | | |
| & Revised | | |
| Passwords | | |
| Company/Product | URL | Log-in |
| | | |
| Password | | |
| & Revised | | |
| Passwords | | |
| Company/Product | URL | Log-in |
| | | |
| Password | | |
| & Revised | | |
| Passwords | | |
| Company/Product | URL | Log-in |
| | | |
| Password | | |
| & Revised | | |
| Passwords | | |

| Company/Product | URL | Log-in |
|---|---|---|
|  |  |  |

| Password | | | |
|---|---|---|---|
| & Revised | | | |
| Passwords | | | |

| Company/Product | URL | Log-in |
|---|---|---|
|  |  |  |

| Password | | | |
|---|---|---|---|
| & Revised | | | |
| Passwords | | | |

| Company/Product | URL | Log-in |
|---|---|---|
|  |  |  |

| Password | | | |
|---|---|---|---|
| & Revised | | | |
| Passwords | | | |

| Company/Product | URL | Log-in |
|---|---|---|
|  |  |  |

| Password | | | |
|---|---|---|---|
| & Revised | | | |
| Passwords | | | |

# C

| Company/Product | URL | Log-in |
| --- | --- | --- |
|  |  |  |

| Password |  |  |  |
| --- | --- | --- | --- |
| & Revised |  |  |  |
| Passwords |  |  |  |

| Company/Product | URL | Log-in |
| --- | --- | --- |
|  |  |  |

| Password |  |  |  |
| --- | --- | --- | --- |
| & Revised |  |  |  |
| Passwords |  |  |  |

| Company/Product | URL | Log-in |
| --- | --- | --- |
|  |  |  |

| Password |  |  |  |
| --- | --- | --- | --- |
| & Revised |  |  |  |
| Passwords |  |  |  |

| Company/Product | URL | Log-in |
| --- | --- | --- |
|  |  |  |

| Password |  |  |  |
| --- | --- | --- | --- |
| & Revised |  |  |  |
| Passwords |  |  |  |

| Company/Product | URL | Log-in |
| --- | --- | --- |
| | | |

| Password | | | |
| --- | --- | --- | --- |
| & Revised | | | |
| Passwords | | | |

| Company/Product | URL | Log-in |
| --- | --- | --- |
| | | |

| Password | | | |
| --- | --- | --- | --- |
| & Revised | | | |
| Passwords | | | |

| Company/Product | URL | Log-in |
| --- | --- | --- |
| | | |

| Password | | | |
| --- | --- | --- | --- |
| & Revised | | | |
| Passwords | | | |

| Company/Product | URL | Log-in |
| --- | --- | --- |
| | | |

| Password | | | |
| --- | --- | --- | --- |
| & Revised | | | |
| Passwords | | | |

| Company/Product | | URL | | Log-in | |
| --- | --- | --- | --- | --- | --- |
| | | | | | |
| Password | | | | | |
| & Revised | | | | | |
| Passwords | | | | | |
| Company/Product | | URL | | Log-in | |
| | | | | | |
| Password | | | | | |
| & Revised | | | | | |
| Passwords | | | | | |
| Company/Product | | URL | | Log-in | |
| | | | | | |
| Password | | | | | |
| & Revised | | | | | |
| Passwords | | | | | |
| Company/Product | | URL | | Log-in | |
| | | | | | |
| Password | | | | | |
| & Revised | | | | | |
| Passwords | | | | | |

| Company/Product | URL | Log-in |
| --- | --- | --- |
|  |  |  |

| Password | | | |
| --- | --- | --- | --- |
| & Revised | | | |
| Passwords | | | |

| Company/Product | URL | Log-in |
| --- | --- | --- |
|  |  |  |

| Password | | | |
| --- | --- | --- | --- |
| & Revised | | | |
| Passwords | | | |

| Company/Product | URL | Log-in |
| --- | --- | --- |
|  |  |  |

| Password | | | |
| --- | --- | --- | --- |
| & Revised | | | |
| Passwords | | | |

| Company/Product | URL | Log-in |
| --- | --- | --- |
|  |  |  |

| Password | | | |
| --- | --- | --- | --- |
| & Revised | | | |
| Passwords | | | |

| Company/Product | URL | Log-in |
|---|---|---|
| | | |

| Password | | | |
|---|---|---|---|
| & Revised | | | |
| Passwords | | | |

| Company/Product | URL | Log-in |
|---|---|---|
| | | |

| Password | | | |
|---|---|---|---|
| & Revised | | | |
| Passwords | | | |

| Company/Product | URL | Log-in |
|---|---|---|
| | | |

| Password | | | |
|---|---|---|---|
| & Revised | | | |
| Passwords | | | |

| Company/Product | URL | Log-in |
|---|---|---|
| | | |

| Password | | | |
|---|---|---|---|
| & Revised | | | |
| Passwords | | | |

| Company/Product | | URL | Log-in |
| --- | --- | --- | --- |
| | | | |
| Password | | | |
| & Revised | | | |
| Passwords | | | |
| Company/Product | | URL | Log-in |
| | | | |
| Password | | | |
| & Revised | | | |
| Passwords | | | |
| Company/Product | | URL | Log-in |
| | | | |
| Password | | | |
| & Revised | | | |
| Passwords | | | |
| Company/Product | | URL | Log-in |
| | | | |
| Password | | | |
| & Revised | | | |
| Passwords | | | |

# D

| Company/Product | URL | Log-in |
| --- | --- | --- |
|  |  |  |

| Password |  |  |  |
| --- | --- | --- | --- |
| & Revised |  |  |  |
| Passwords |  |  |  |

| Company/Product | URL | Log-in |
| --- | --- | --- |
|  |  |  |

| Password |  |  |  |
| --- | --- | --- | --- |
| & Revised |  |  |  |
| Passwords |  |  |  |

| Company/Product | URL | Log-in |
| --- | --- | --- |
|  |  |  |

| Password |  |  |  |
| --- | --- | --- | --- |
| & Revised |  |  |  |
| Passwords |  |  |  |

| Company/Product | URL | Log-in |
| --- | --- | --- |
|  |  |  |

| Password |  |  |  |
| --- | --- | --- | --- |
| & Revised |  |  |  |
| Passwords |  |  |  |

| Company/Product | URL | Log-in |
| --- | --- | --- |
|  |  |  |
| Password |  |  |  |
| & Revised |  |  |  |
| Passwords |  |  |  |

| Company/Product | URL | Log-in |
| --- | --- | --- |
|  |  |  |
| Password |  |  |  |
| & Revised |  |  |  |
| Passwords |  |  |  |

| Company/Product | URL | Log-in |
| --- | --- | --- |
|  |  |  |
| Password |  |  |  |
| & Revised |  |  |  |
| Passwords |  |  |  |

| Company/Product | URL | Log-in |
| --- | --- | --- |
|  |  |  |
| Password |  |  |  |
| & Revised |  |  |  |
| Passwords |  |  |  |

| Company/Product | URL | Log-in |
| --- | --- | --- |
|  |  |  |
| Password |  |  |  |
| & Revised |  |  |  |
| Passwords |  |  |  |
| Company/Product | URL | Log-in |
|  |  |  |
| Password |  |  |  |
| & Revised |  |  |  |
| Passwords |  |  |  |
| Company/Product | URL | Log-in |
|  |  |  |
| Password |  |  |  |
| & Revised |  |  |  |
| Passwords |  |  |  |
| Company/Product | URL | Log-in |
|  |  |  |
| Password |  |  |  |
| & Revised |  |  |  |
| Passwords |  |  |  |

| Company/Product | URL | Log-in |
| --- | --- | --- |
|  |  |  |
| Password | | |
| & Revised | | |
| Passwords | | |
| Company/Product | URL | Log-in |
|  |  |  |
| Password | | |
| & Revised | | |
| Passwords | | |
| Company/Product | URL | Log-in |
|  |  |  |
| Password | | |
| & Revised | | |
| Passwords | | |
| Company/Product | URL | Log-in |
|  |  |  |
| Password | | |
| & Revised | | |
| Passwords | | |

# E

| Company/Product | URL | Log-in |
| --- | --- | --- |
|  |  |  |

| Password |  |  |  |
| --- | --- | --- | --- |
| & Revised |  |  |  |
| Passwords |  |  |  |

| Company/Product | URL | Log-in |
| --- | --- | --- |
|  |  |  |

| Password |  |  |  |
| --- | --- | --- | --- |
| & Revised |  |  |  |
| Passwords |  |  |  |

| Company/Product | URL | Log-in |
| --- | --- | --- |
|  |  |  |

| Password |  |  |  |
| --- | --- | --- | --- |
| & Revised |  |  |  |
| Passwords |  |  |  |

| Company/Product | URL | Log-in |
| --- | --- | --- |
|  |  |  |

| Password |  |  |  |
| --- | --- | --- | --- |
| & Revised |  |  |  |
| Passwords |  |  |  |

| Company/Product | URL | Log-in |
|---|---|---|
|  |  |  |

| Password | | | |
|---|---|---|---|
| & Revised | | | |
| Passwords | | | |

| Company/Product | URL | Log-in |
|---|---|---|
|  |  |  |

| Password | | | |
|---|---|---|---|
| & Revised | | | |
| Passwords | | | |

| Company/Product | URL | Log-in |
|---|---|---|
|  |  |  |

| Password | | | |
|---|---|---|---|
| & Revised | | | |
| Passwords | | | |

| Company/Product | URL | Log-in |
|---|---|---|
|  |  |  |

| Password | | | |
|---|---|---|---|
| & Revised | | | |
| Passwords | | | |

| Company/Product | URL | Log-in |
| --- | --- | --- |
| | | |
| Password | | |
| & Revised | | |
| Passwords | | |
| Company/Product | URL | Log-in |
| | | |
| Password | | |
| & Revised | | |
| Passwords | | |
| Company/Product | URL | Log-in |
| | | |
| Password | | |
| & Revised | | |
| Passwords | | |
| Company/Product | URL | Log-in |
| | | |
| Password | | |
| & Revised | | |
| Passwords | | |

| Company/Product | URL | Log-in |
| --- | --- | --- |
|  |  |  |
| Password | | |
| & Revised | | |
| Passwords | | |
| Company/Product | URL | Log-in |
|  |  |  |
| Password | | |
| & Revised | | |
| Passwords | | |
| Company/Product | URL | Log-in |
|  |  |  |
| Password | | |
| & Revised | | |
| Passwords | | |
| Company/Product | URL | Log-in |
|  |  |  |
| Password | | |
| & Revised | | |
| Passwords | | |

# F

| Company/Product | URL | Log-in |
| --- | --- | --- |
|  |  |  |
| Password |  |  |
| & Revised |  |  |
| Passwords |  |  |
| Company/Product | URL | Log-in |
|  |  |  |
| Password |  |  |
| & Revised |  |  |
| Passwords |  |  |
| Company/Product | URL | Log-in |
|  |  |  |
| Password |  |  |
| & Revised |  |  |
| Passwords |  |  |
| Company/Product | URL | Log-in |
|  |  |  |
| Password |  |  |
| & Revised |  |  |
| Passwords |  |  |

| Company/Product | URL | Log-in |
| --- | --- | --- |
|  |  |  |

| Password | | | |
| --- | --- | --- | --- |
| & Revised | | | |
| Passwords | | | |

| Company/Product | URL | Log-in |
| --- | --- | --- |
|  |  |  |

| Password | | | |
| --- | --- | --- | --- |
| & Revised | | | |
| Passwords | | | |

| Company/Product | URL | Log-in |
| --- | --- | --- |
|  |  |  |

| Password | | | |
| --- | --- | --- | --- |
| & Revised | | | |
| Passwords | | | |

| Company/Product | URL | Log-in |
| --- | --- | --- |
|  |  |  |

| Password | | | |
| --- | --- | --- | --- |
| & Revised | | | |
| Passwords | | | |

| Company/Product | URL | Log-in |
|---|---|---|
| | | |
| **Password** | | | |
| **& Revised** | | | |
| **Passwords** | | | |
| Company/Product | URL | Log-in |
| | | |
| **Password** | | | |
| **& Revised** | | | |
| **Passwords** | | | |
| Company/Product | URL | Log-in |
| | | |
| **Password** | | | |
| **& Revised** | | | |
| **Passwords** | | | |
| Company/Product | URL | Log-in |
| | | |
| **Password** | | | |
| **& Revised** | | | |
| **Passwords** | | | |

| Company/Product | URL | Log-in |
| --- | --- | --- |
| | | |
| Password | | | |
| & Revised | | | |
| Passwords | | | |
| Company/Product | URL | Log-in |
| | | |
| Password | | | |
| & Revised | | | |
| Passwords | | | |
| Company/Product | URL | Log-in |
| | | |
| Password | | | |
| & Revised | | | |
| Passwords | | | |
| Company/Product | URL | Log-in |
| | | |
| Password | | | |
| & Revised | | | |
| Passwords | | | |

# G

| Company/Product | URL | Log-in |
| --- | --- | --- |
|  |  |  |

| Password |  |  |  |
| --- | --- | --- | --- |
| & Revised |  |  |  |
| Passwords |  |  |  |

| Company/Product | URL | Log-in |
| --- | --- | --- |
|  |  |  |

| Password |  |  |  |
| --- | --- | --- | --- |
| & Revised |  |  |  |
| Passwords |  |  |  |

| Company/Product | URL | Log-in |
| --- | --- | --- |
|  |  |  |

| Password |  |  |  |
| --- | --- | --- | --- |
| & Revised |  |  |  |
| Passwords |  |  |  |

| Company/Product | URL | Log-in |
| --- | --- | --- |
|  |  |  |

| Password |  |  |  |
| --- | --- | --- | --- |
| & Revised |  |  |  |
| Passwords |  |  |  |

| Company/Product | URL | Log-in |
|---|---|---|
|  |  |  |
| Password & Revised Passwords |  |  |

| Company/Product | URL | Log-in |
|---|---|---|
|  |  |  |
| Password & Revised Passwords |  |  |

| Company/Product | URL | Log-in |
|---|---|---|
|  |  |  |
| Password & Revised Passwords |  |  |

| Company/Product | URL | Log-in |
|---|---|---|
|  |  |  |
| Password & Revised Passwords |  |  |

| Company/Product | URL | Log-in |
| --- | --- | --- |
| | | |
| Password | | |
| & Revised | | |
| Passwords | | |
| Company/Product | URL | Log-in |
| | | |
| Password | | |
| & Revised | | |
| Passwords | | |
| Company/Product | URL | Log-in |
| | | |
| Password | | |
| & Revised | | |
| Passwords | | |
| Company/Product | URL | Log-in |
| | | |
| Password | | |
| & Revised | | |
| Passwords | | |

| Company/Product | URL | Log-in |
| --- | --- | --- |
| | | |

| Password | | | |
| --- | --- | --- | --- |
| & Revised | | | |
| Passwords | | | |

| Company/Product | URL | Log-in |
| --- | --- | --- |
| | | |

| Password | | | |
| --- | --- | --- | --- |
| & Revised | | | |
| Passwords | | | |

| Company/Product | URL | Log-in |
| --- | --- | --- |
| | | |

| Password | | | |
| --- | --- | --- | --- |
| & Revised | | | |
| Passwords | | | |

| Company/Product | URL | Log-in |
| --- | --- | --- |
| | | |

| Password | | | |
| --- | --- | --- | --- |
| & Revised | | | |
| Passwords | | | |

# H

| Company/Product | URL | Log-in |
| --- | --- | --- |
| | | |

| Password | | | |
| --- | --- | --- | --- |
| & Revised | | | |
| Passwords | | | |

| Company/Product | URL | Log-in |
| --- | --- | --- |
| | | |

| Password | | | |
| --- | --- | --- | --- |
| & Revised | | | |
| Passwords | | | |

| Company/Product | URL | Log-in |
| --- | --- | --- |
| | | |

| Password | | | |
| --- | --- | --- | --- |
| & Revised | | | |
| Passwords | | | |

| Company/Product | URL | Log-in |
| --- | --- | --- |
| | | |

| Password | | | |
| --- | --- | --- | --- |
| & Revised | | | |
| Passwords | | | |

| Company/Product | URL | Log-in |
| --- | --- | --- |
|  |  |  |
| Password | | |
| & Revised | | |
| Passwords | | |
| Company/Product | URL | Log-in |
|  |  |  |
| Password | | |
| & Revised | | |
| Passwords | | |
| Company/Product | URL | Log-in |
|  |  |  |
| Password | | |
| & Revised | | |
| Passwords | | |
| Company/Product | URL | Log-in |
|  |  |  |
| Password | | |
| & Revised | | |
| Passwords | | |

| Company/Product | URL | Log-in |
| --- | --- | --- |
|  |  |  |
| Password | | |
| & Revised | | |
| Passwords | | |
| Company/Product | URL | Log-in |
|  |  |  |
| Password | | |
| & Revised | | |
| Passwords | | |
| Company/Product | URL | Log-in |
|  |  |  |
| Password | | |
| & Revised | | |
| Passwords | | |
| Company/Product | URL | Log-in |
|  |  |  |
| Password | | |
| & Revised | | |
| Passwords | | |

| Company/Product | URL | Log-in |
| --- | --- | --- |
| | | |
| Password | | |
| & Revised | | |
| Passwords | | |
| Company/Product | URL | Log-in |
| | | |
| Password | | |
| & Revised | | |
| Passwords | | |
| Company/Product | URL | Log-in |
| | | |
| Password | | |
| & Revised | | |
| Passwords | | |
| Company/Product | URL | Log-in |
| | | |
| Password | | |
| & Revised | | |
| Passwords | | |

| Company/Product | URL | Log-in |
|---|---|---|
| | | |
| Password | | | |
| & Revised | | | |
| Passwords | | | |
| Company/Product | URL | Log-in |
| | | |
| Password | | | |
| & Revised | | | |
| Passwords | | | |
| Company/Product | URL | Log-in |
| | | |
| Password | | | |
| & Revised | | | |
| Passwords | | | |
| Company/Product | URL | Log-in |
| | | |
| Password | | | |
| & Revised | | | |
| Passwords | | | |

| Company/Product | URL | Log-in |
| --- | --- | --- |
| | | |
| Password | | | |
| & Revised | | | |
| Passwords | | | |

| Company/Product | URL | Log-in |
| --- | --- | --- |
| | | |
| Password | | | |
| & Revised | | | |
| Passwords | | | |

| Company/Product | URL | Log-in |
| --- | --- | --- |
| | | |
| Password | | | |
| & Revised | | | |
| Passwords | | | |

| Company/Product | URL | Log-in |
| --- | --- | --- |
| | | |
| Password | | | |
| & Revised | | | |
| Passwords | | | |

| Company/Product | URL | Log-in |
|---|---|---|
|  |  |  |
| Password |  |  |  |
| & Revised |  |  |  |
| Passwords |  |  |  |
| Company/Product | URL | Log-in |
|  |  |  |
| Password |  |  |  |
| & Revised |  |  |  |
| Passwords |  |  |  |
| Company/Product | URL | Log-in |
|  |  |  |
| Password |  |  |  |
| & Revised |  |  |  |
| Passwords |  |  |  |
| Company/Product | URL | Log-in |
|  |  |  |
| Password |  |  |  |
| & Revised |  |  |  |
| Passwords |  |  |  |

| Company/Product | URL | Log-in |
| --- | --- | --- |
| | | |

| Password | | | |
| --- | --- | --- | --- |
| & Revised | | | |
| Passwords | | | |

| Company/Product | URL | Log-in |
| --- | --- | --- |
| | | |

| Password | | | |
| --- | --- | --- | --- |
| & Revised | | | |
| Passwords | | | |

| Company/Product | URL | Log-in |
| --- | --- | --- |
| | | |

| Password | | | |
| --- | --- | --- | --- |
| & Revised | | | |
| Passwords | | | |

| Company/Product | URL | Log-in |
| --- | --- | --- |
| | | |

| Password | | | |
| --- | --- | --- | --- |
| & Revised | | | |
| Passwords | | | |

| Company/Product | URL | Log-in |
| --- | --- | --- |
| | | |
| Password | | |
| & Revised | | |
| Passwords | | |
| Company/Product | URL | Log-in |
| | | |
| Password | | |
| & Revised | | |
| Passwords | | |
| Company/Product | URL | Log-in |
| | | |
| Password | | |
| & Revised | | |
| Passwords | | |
| Company/Product | URL | Log-in |
| | | |
| Password | | |
| & Revised | | |
| Passwords | | |

| Company/Product | URL | Log-in |
| --- | --- | --- |
|  |  |  |
| **Password** |  |  |  |
| **& Revised** |  |  |  |
| **Passwords** |  |  |  |
| Company/Product | URL | Log-in |
|  |  |  |
| **Password** |  |  |  |
| **& Revised** |  |  |  |
| **Passwords** |  |  |  |
| Company/Product | URL | Log-in |
|  |  |  |
| **Password** |  |  |  |
| **& Revised** |  |  |  |
| **Passwords** |  |  |  |
| Company/Product | URL | Log-in |
|  |  |  |
| **Password** |  |  |  |
| **& Revised** |  |  |  |
| **Passwords** |  |  |  |

# K

| Company/Product | URL | Log-in |
| --- | --- | --- |
|  |  |  |

| Password | | | |
| --- | --- | --- | --- |
| & Revised | | | |
| Passwords | | | |

| Company/Product | URL | Log-in |
| --- | --- | --- |
|  |  |  |

| Password | | | |
| --- | --- | --- | --- |
| & Revised | | | |
| Passwords | | | |

| Company/Product | URL | Log-in |
| --- | --- | --- |
|  |  |  |

| Password | | | |
| --- | --- | --- | --- |
| & Revised | | | |
| Passwords | | | |

| Company/Product | URL | Log-in |
| --- | --- | --- |
|  |  |  |

| Password | | | |
| --- | --- | --- | --- |
| & Revised | | | |
| Passwords | | | |

| Company/Product | | URL | Log-in |
|---|---|---|---|
| | | | |
| Password | | | |
| & Revised | | | |
| Passwords | | | |
| Company/Product | | URL | Log-in |
| | | | |
| Password | | | |
| & Revised | | | |
| Passwords | | | |
| Company/Product | | URL | Log-in |
| | | | |
| Password | | | |
| & Revised | | | |
| Passwords | | | |
| Company/Product | | URL | Log-in |
| | | | |
| Password | | | |
| & Revised | | | |
| Passwords | | | |

| Company/Product | URL | Log-in |
| --- | --- | --- |
|  |  |  |
| Password |  |  |  |
| & Revised |  |  |  |
| Passwords |  |  |  |
| Company/Product | URL | Log-in |
|  |  |  |
| Password |  |  |  |
| & Revised |  |  |  |
| Passwords |  |  |  |
| Company/Product | URL | Log-in |
|  |  |  |
| Password |  |  |  |
| & Revised |  |  |  |
| Passwords |  |  |  |
| Company/Product | URL | Log-in |
|  |  |  |
| Password |  |  |  |
| & Revised |  |  |  |
| Passwords |  |  |  |

| Company/Product | URL | Log-in |
| --- | --- | --- |
|  |  |  |

| Password |  |  |  |
| --- | --- | --- | --- |
| & Revised |  |  |  |
| Passwords |  |  |  |

| Company/Product | URL | Log-in |
| --- | --- | --- |
|  |  |  |

| Password |  |  |  |
| --- | --- | --- | --- |
| & Revised |  |  |  |
| Passwords |  |  |  |

| Company/Product | URL | Log-in |
| --- | --- | --- |
|  |  |  |

| Password |  |  |  |
| --- | --- | --- | --- |
| & Revised |  |  |  |
| Passwords |  |  |  |

| Company/Product | URL | Log-in |
| --- | --- | --- |
|  |  |  |

| Password |  |  |  |
| --- | --- | --- | --- |
| & Revised |  |  |  |
| Passwords |  |  |  |

# L

| Company/Product | URL | Log-in |
| --- | --- | --- |
|  |  |  |

| Password | | | |
| --- | --- | --- | --- |
| & Revised | | | |
| Passwords | | | |

| Company/Product | URL | Log-in |
| --- | --- | --- |
|  |  |  |

| Password | | | |
| --- | --- | --- | --- |
| & Revised | | | |
| Passwords | | | |

| Company/Product | URL | Log-in |
| --- | --- | --- |
|  |  |  |

| Password | | | |
| --- | --- | --- | --- |
| & Revised | | | |
| Passwords | | | |

| Company/Product | URL | Log-in |
| --- | --- | --- |
|  |  |  |

| Password | | | |
| --- | --- | --- | --- |
| & Revised | | | |
| Passwords | | | |

| Company/Product | | URL | Log-in |
| --- | --- | --- | --- |
| | | | |
| **Password** | | | |
| **& Revised** | | | |
| **Passwords** | | | |
| Company/Product | | URL | Log-in |
| | | | |
| **Password** | | | |
| **& Revised** | | | |
| **Passwords** | | | |
| Company/Product | | URL | Log-in |
| | | | |
| **Password** | | | |
| **& Revised** | | | |
| **Passwords** | | | |
| Company/Product | | URL | Log-in |
| | | | |
| **Password** | | | |
| **& Revised** | | | |
| **Passwords** | | | |

| Company/Product | URL | Log-in |
| --- | --- | --- |
| | | |
| **Password & Revised Passwords** | | |
| Company/Product | URL | Log-in |
| | | |
| **Password & Revised Passwords** | | |
| Company/Product | URL | Log-in |
| | | |
| **Password & Revised Passwords** | | |
| Company/Product | URL | Log-in |
| | | |
| **Password & Revised Passwords** | | |

| Company/Product | | URL | Log-in |
| --- | --- | --- | --- |
| | | | |
| Password | | | |
| & Revised | | | |
| Passwords | | | |
| Company/Product | | URL | Log-in |
| | | | |
| Password | | | |
| & Revised | | | |
| Passwords | | | |
| Company/Product | | URL | Log-in |
| | | | |
| Password | | | |
| & Revised | | | |
| Passwords | | | |
| Company/Product | | URL | Log-in |
| | | | |
| Password | | | |
| & Revised | | | |
| Passwords | | | |

# M

| Company/Product | URL | Log-in |
| --- | --- | --- |
|  |  |  |

| Password |  |  |  |
| --- | --- | --- | --- |
| & Revised |  |  |  |
| Passwords |  |  |  |

| Company/Product | URL | Log-in |
| --- | --- | --- |
|  |  |  |

| Password |  |  |  |
| --- | --- | --- | --- |
| & Revised |  |  |  |
| Passwords |  |  |  |

| Company/Product | URL | Log-in |
| --- | --- | --- |
|  |  |  |

| Password |  |  |  |
| --- | --- | --- | --- |
| & Revised |  |  |  |
| Passwords |  |  |  |

| Company/Product | URL | Log-in |
| --- | --- | --- |
|  |  |  |

| Password |  |  |  |
| --- | --- | --- | --- |
| & Revised |  |  |  |
| Passwords |  |  |  |

| Company/Product | URL | Log-in |
| --- | --- | --- |
|  |  |  |
| Password |  |  |  |
| & Revised |  |  |  |
| Passwords |  |  |  |

| Company/Product | URL | Log-in |
| --- | --- | --- |
|  |  |  |
| Password |  |  |  |
| & Revised |  |  |  |
| Passwords |  |  |  |

| Company/Product | URL | Log-in |
| --- | --- | --- |
|  |  |  |
| Password |  |  |  |
| & Revised |  |  |  |
| Passwords |  |  |  |

| Company/Product | URL | Log-in |
| --- | --- | --- |
|  |  |  |
| Password |  |  |  |
| & Revised |  |  |  |
| Passwords |  |  |  |

| Company/Product | URL | Log-in |
|---|---|---|
|  |  |  |

| Password |  |  |  |
|---|---|---|---|
| & Revised |  |  |  |
| Passwords |  |  |  |

| Company/Product | URL | Log-in |
|---|---|---|
|  |  |  |

| Password |  |  |  |
|---|---|---|---|
| & Revised |  |  |  |
| Passwords |  |  |  |

| Company/Product | URL | Log-in |
|---|---|---|
|  |  |  |

| Password |  |  |  |
|---|---|---|---|
| & Revised |  |  |  |
| Passwords |  |  |  |

| Company/Product | URL | Log-in |
|---|---|---|
|  |  |  |

| Password |  |  |  |
|---|---|---|---|
| & Revised |  |  |  |
| Passwords |  |  |  |

| Company/Product | URL | Log-in |
| --- | --- | --- |
|  |  |  |

| Password |  |  |  |
| --- | --- | --- | --- |
| & Revised |  |  |  |
| Passwords |  |  |  |

| Company/Product | URL | Log-in |
| --- | --- | --- |
|  |  |  |

| Password |  |  |  |
| --- | --- | --- | --- |
| & Revised |  |  |  |
| Passwords |  |  |  |

| Company/Product | URL | Log-in |
| --- | --- | --- |
|  |  |  |

| Password |  |  |  |
| --- | --- | --- | --- |
| & Revised |  |  |  |
| Passwords |  |  |  |

| Company/Product | URL | Log-in |
| --- | --- | --- |
|  |  |  |

| Password |  |  |  |
| --- | --- | --- | --- |
| & Revised |  |  |  |
| Passwords |  |  |  |

| Company/Product | URL | Log-in |
| --- | --- | --- |
|  |  |  |
| **Password** |  |  |  |
| **& Revised** |  |  |  |
| **Passwords** |  |  |  |
| **Company/Product** | **URL** | **Log-in** |
|  |  |  |
| **Password** |  |  |  |
| **& Revised** |  |  |  |
| **Passwords** |  |  |  |
| **Company/Product** | **URL** | **Log-in** |
|  |  |  |
| **Password** |  |  |  |
| **& Revised** |  |  |  |
| **Passwords** |  |  |  |
| **Company/Product** | **URL** | **Log-in** |
|  |  |  |
| **Password** |  |  |  |
| **& Revised** |  |  |  |
| **Passwords** |  |  |  |

| Company/Product | URL | Log-in |
| --- | --- | --- |
|  |  |  |
| Password |  |  |  |
| & Revised |  |  |  |
| Passwords |  |  |  |

| Company/Product | URL | Log-in |
| --- | --- | --- |
|  |  |  |
| Password |  |  |  |
| & Revised |  |  |  |
| Passwords |  |  |  |

| Company/Product | URL | Log-in |
| --- | --- | --- |
|  |  |  |
| Password |  |  |  |
| & Revised |  |  |  |
| Passwords |  |  |  |

| Company/Product | URL | Log-in |
| --- | --- | --- |
|  |  |  |
| Password |  |  |  |
| & Revised |  |  |  |
| Passwords |  |  |  |

# N

| Company/Product | URL | Log-in |
| --- | --- | --- |
|  |  |  |
| **Password** |  |  |
| **& Revised** |  |  |
| **Passwords** |  |  |

| Company/Product | URL | Log-in |
| --- | --- | --- |
|  |  |  |
| **Password** |  |  |
| **& Revised** |  |  |
| **Passwords** |  |  |

| Company/Product | URL | Log-in |
| --- | --- | --- |
|  |  |  |
| **Password** |  |  |
| **& Revised** |  |  |
| **Passwords** |  |  |

| Company/Product | URL | Log-in |
| --- | --- | --- |
|  |  |  |
| **Password** |  |  |
| **& Revised** |  |  |
| **Passwords** |  |  |

| Company/Product | URL | Log-in |
| --- | --- | --- |
|  |  |  |

| Password | | | |
| --- | --- | --- | --- |
| & Revised | | | |
| Passwords | | | |

| Company/Product | URL | Log-in |
| --- | --- | --- |
|  |  |  |

| Password | | | |
| --- | --- | --- | --- |
| & Revised | | | |
| Passwords | | | |

| Company/Product | URL | Log-in |
| --- | --- | --- |
|  |  |  |

| Password | | | |
| --- | --- | --- | --- |
| & Revised | | | |
| Passwords | | | |

| Company/Product | URL | Log-in |
| --- | --- | --- |
|  |  |  |

| Password | | | |
| --- | --- | --- | --- |
| & Revised | | | |
| Passwords | | | |

| Company/Product | URL | Log-in |
| --- | --- | --- |
|  |  |  |
| **Password** |  |  |  |
| **& Revised** |  |  |  |
| **Passwords** |  |  |  |
| **Company/Product** | **URL** | **Log-in** |
|  |  |  |
| **Password** |  |  |  |
| **& Revised** |  |  |  |
| **Passwords** |  |  |  |
| **Company/Product** | **URL** | **Log-in** |
|  |  |  |
| **Password** |  |  |  |
| **& Revised** |  |  |  |
| **Passwords** |  |  |  |
| **Company/Product** | **URL** | **Log-in** |
|  |  |  |
| **Password** |  |  |  |
| **& Revised** |  |  |  |
| **Passwords** |  |  |  |

| Company/Product | URL | Log-in |
| --- | --- | --- |
| | | |

| Password | | | |
| --- | --- | --- | --- |
| & Revised | | | |
| Passwords | | | |

| Company/Product | URL | Log-in |
| --- | --- | --- |
| | | |

| Password | | | |
| --- | --- | --- | --- |
| & Revised | | | |
| Passwords | | | |

| Company/Product | URL | Log-in |
| --- | --- | --- |
| | | |

| Password | | | |
| --- | --- | --- | --- |
| & Revised | | | |
| Passwords | | | |

| Company/Product | URL | Log-in |
| --- | --- | --- |
| | | |

| Password | | | |
| --- | --- | --- | --- |
| & Revised | | | |
| Passwords | | | |

# O

| Company/Product | URL | Log-in |
|---|---|---|
|  |  |  |

| Password | | | |
|---|---|---|---|
| & Revised | | | |
| Passwords | | | |

| Company/Product | URL | Log-in |
|---|---|---|
|  |  |  |

| Password | | | |
|---|---|---|---|
| & Revised | | | |
| Passwords | | | |

| Company/Product | URL | Log-in |
|---|---|---|
|  |  |  |

| Password | | | |
|---|---|---|---|
| & Revised | | | |
| Passwords | | | |

| Company/Product | URL | Log-in |
|---|---|---|
|  |  |  |

| Password | | | |
|---|---|---|---|
| & Revised | | | |
| Passwords | | | |

| Company/Product | URL | Log-in |
| --- | --- | --- |
| | | |
| **Password** | | | |
| **& Revised** | | | |
| **Passwords** | | | |

| Company/Product | URL | Log-in |
| --- | --- | --- |
| | | |
| **Password** | | | |
| **& Revised** | | | |
| **Passwords** | | | |

| Company/Product | URL | Log-in |
| --- | --- | --- |
| | | |
| **Password** | | | |
| **& Revised** | | | |
| **Passwords** | | | |

| Company/Product | URL | Log-in |
| --- | --- | --- |
| | | |
| **Password** | | | |
| **& Revised** | | | |
| **Passwords** | | | |

| Company/Product | URL | Log-in |
| --- | --- | --- |
|  |  |  |
| Password |  |  |  |
| & Revised |  |  |  |
| Passwords |  |  |  |
| Company/Product | URL | Log-in |
|  |  |  |
| Password |  |  |  |
| & Revised |  |  |  |
| Passwords |  |  |  |
| Company/Product | URL | Log-in |
|  |  |  |
| Password |  |  |  |
| & Revised |  |  |  |
| Passwords |  |  |  |
| Company/Product | URL | Log-in |
|  |  |  |
| Password |  |  |  |
| & Revised |  |  |  |
| Passwords |  |  |  |

| Company/Product | URL | Log-in |
| --- | --- | --- |
|  |  |  |
| Password |  |  |  |
| & Revised |  |  |  |
| Passwords |  |  |  |
| Company/Product | URL | Log-in |
|  |  |  |
| Password |  |  |  |
| & Revised |  |  |  |
| Passwords |  |  |  |
| Company/Product | URL | Log-in |
|  |  |  |
| Password |  |  |  |
| & Revised |  |  |  |
| Passwords |  |  |  |
| Company/Product | URL | Log-in |
|  |  |  |
| Password |  |  |  |
| & Revised |  |  |  |
| Passwords |  |  |  |

# P

| Company/Product | | URL | Log-in |
| --- | --- | --- | --- |
| | | | |
| Password | | | |
| & Revised | | | |
| Passwords | | | |
| Company/Product | | URL | Log-in |
| | | | |
| Password | | | |
| & Revised | | | |
| Passwords | | | |
| Company/Product | | URL | Log-in |
| | | | |
| Password | | | |
| & Revised | | | |
| Passwords | | | |
| Company/Product | | URL | Log-in |
| | | | |
| Password | | | |
| & Revised | | | |
| Passwords | | | |

| Company/Product | URL | Log-in |
| --- | --- | --- |
| | | |

| Password | | | |
| --- | --- | --- | --- |
| & Revised | | | |
| Passwords | | | |

| Company/Product | URL | Log-in |
| --- | --- | --- |
| | | |

| Password | | | |
| --- | --- | --- | --- |
| & Revised | | | |
| Passwords | | | |

| Company/Product | URL | Log-in |
| --- | --- | --- |
| | | |

| Password | | | |
| --- | --- | --- | --- |
| & Revised | | | |
| Passwords | | | |

| Company/Product | URL | Log-in |
| --- | --- | --- |
| | | |

| Password | | | |
| --- | --- | --- | --- |
| & Revised | | | |
| Passwords | | | |

| Company/Product | URL | Log-in |
| --- | --- | --- |
|  |  |  |

| Password | | | |
| --- | --- | --- | --- |
| & Revised | | | |
| Passwords | | | |

| Company/Product | URL | Log-in |
| --- | --- | --- |
|  |  |  |

| Password | | | |
| --- | --- | --- | --- |
| & Revised | | | |
| Passwords | | | |

| Company/Product | URL | Log-in |
| --- | --- | --- |
|  |  |  |

| Password | | | |
| --- | --- | --- | --- |
| & Revised | | | |
| Passwords | | | |

| Company/Product | URL | Log-in |
| --- | --- | --- |
|  |  |  |

| Password | | | |
| --- | --- | --- | --- |
| & Revised | | | |
| Passwords | | | |

| Company/Product | URL | Log-in |
|---|---|---|
|  |  |  |

| Password |  |  |  |
|---|---|---|---|
| & Revised |  |  |  |
| Passwords |  |  |  |

| Company/Product | URL | Log-in |
|---|---|---|
|  |  |  |

| Password |  |  |  |
|---|---|---|---|
| & Revised |  |  |  |
| Passwords |  |  |  |

| Company/Product | URL | Log-in |
|---|---|---|
|  |  |  |

| Password |  |  |  |
|---|---|---|---|
| & Revised |  |  |  |
| Passwords |  |  |  |

| Company/Product | URL | Log-in |
|---|---|---|
|  |  |  |

| Password |  |  |  |
|---|---|---|---|
| & Revised |  |  |  |
| Passwords |  |  |  |

# Q

| Company/Product | URL | Log-in |
| --- | --- | --- |
| | | |
| Password | | |
| & Revised | | |
| Passwords | | |
| Company/Product | URL | Log-in |
| | | |
| Password | | |
| & Revised | | |
| Passwords | | |
| Company/Product | URL | Log-in |
| | | |
| Password | | |
| & Revised | | |
| Passwords | | |
| Company/Product | URL | Log-in |
| | | |
| Password | | |
| & Revised | | |
| Passwords | | |

| Company/Product | URL | Log-in |
| --- | --- | --- |
|  |  |  |

| Password |  |  |  |
| --- | --- | --- | --- |
| & Revised |  |  |  |
| Passwords |  |  |  |

| Company/Product | URL | Log-in |
| --- | --- | --- |
|  |  |  |

| Password |  |  |  |
| --- | --- | --- | --- |
| & Revised |  |  |  |
| Passwords |  |  |  |

| Company/Product | URL | Log-in |
| --- | --- | --- |
|  |  |  |

| Password |  |  |  |
| --- | --- | --- | --- |
| & Revised |  |  |  |
| Passwords |  |  |  |

| Company/Product | URL | Log-in |
| --- | --- | --- |
|  |  |  |

| Password |  |  |  |
| --- | --- | --- | --- |
| & Revised |  |  |  |
| Passwords |  |  |  |

# R

| Company/Product | URL | Log-in |
| --- | --- | --- |
| | | |

| Password | | | |
| --- | --- | --- | --- |
| & Revised | | | |
| Passwords | | | |

| Company/Product | URL | Log-in |
| --- | --- | --- |
| | | |

| Password | | | |
| --- | --- | --- | --- |
| & Revised | | | |
| Passwords | | | |

| Company/Product | URL | Log-in |
| --- | --- | --- |
| | | |

| Password | | | |
| --- | --- | --- | --- |
| & Revised | | | |
| Passwords | | | |

| Company/Product | URL | Log-in |
| --- | --- | --- |
| | | |

| Password | | | |
| --- | --- | --- | --- |
| & Revised | | | |
| Passwords | | | |

| Company/Product | URL | Log-in |
|---|---|---|
|  |  |  |

| Password | | | |
|---|---|---|---|
| & Revised | | | |
| Passwords | | | |

| Company/Product | URL | Log-in |
|---|---|---|
|  |  |  |

| Password | | | |
|---|---|---|---|
| & Revised | | | |
| Passwords | | | |

| Company/Product | URL | Log-in |
|---|---|---|
|  |  |  |

| Password | | | |
|---|---|---|---|
| & Revised | | | |
| Passwords | | | |

| Company/Product | URL | Log-in |
|---|---|---|
|  |  |  |

| Password | | | |
|---|---|---|---|
| & Revised | | | |
| Passwords | | | |

| Company/Product | URL | Log-in |
| --- | --- | --- |
|  |  |  |

| Password |  |  |  |
| --- | --- | --- | --- |
| & Revised |  |  |  |
| Passwords |  |  |  |

| Company/Product | URL | Log-in |
| --- | --- | --- |
|  |  |  |

| Password |  |  |  |
| --- | --- | --- | --- |
| & Revised |  |  |  |
| Passwords |  |  |  |

| Company/Product | URL | Log-in |
| --- | --- | --- |
|  |  |  |

| Password |  |  |  |
| --- | --- | --- | --- |
| & Revised |  |  |  |
| Passwords |  |  |  |

| Company/Product | URL | Log-in |
| --- | --- | --- |
|  |  |  |

| Password |  |  |  |
| --- | --- | --- | --- |
| & Revised |  |  |  |
| Passwords |  |  |  |

| Company/Product | URL | Log-in |
| --- | --- | --- |
|  |  |  |
| Password | | |
| & Revised | | |
| Passwords | | |
| Company/Product | URL | Log-in |
|  |  |  |
| Password | | |
| & Revised | | |
| Passwords | | |
| Company/Product | URL | Log-in |
|  |  |  |
| Password | | |
| & Revised | | |
| Passwords | | |
| Company/Product | URL | Log-in |
|  |  |  |
| Password | | |
| & Revised | | |
| Passwords | | |

# S

| Company/Product | URL | Log-in |
| --- | --- | --- |
| | | |

| Password | | | |
| --- | --- | --- | --- |
| & Revised | | | |
| Passwords | | | |

| Company/Product | URL | Log-in |
| --- | --- | --- |
| | | |

| Password | | | |
| --- | --- | --- | --- |
| & Revised | | | |
| Passwords | | | |

| Company/Product | URL | Log-in |
| --- | --- | --- |
| | | |

| Password | | | |
| --- | --- | --- | --- |
| & Revised | | | |
| Passwords | | | |

| Company/Product | URL | Log-in |
| --- | --- | --- |
| | | |

| Password | | | |
| --- | --- | --- | --- |
| & Revised | | | |
| Passwords | | | |

| Company/Product | URL | Log-in |
| --- | --- | --- |
| | | |
| **Password** | | |
| **& Revised** | | |
| **Passwords** | | |
| Company/Product | URL | Log-in |
| | | |
| **Password** | | |
| **& Revised** | | |
| **Passwords** | | |
| Company/Product | URL | Log-in |
| | | |
| **Password** | | |
| **& Revised** | | |
| **Passwords** | | |
| Company/Product | URL | Log-in |
| | | |
| **Password** | | |
| **& Revised** | | |
| **Passwords** | | |

| Company/Product | URL | Log-in |
| --- | --- | --- |
|  |  |  |
| Password | | | |
| & Revised | | | |
| Passwords | | | |
| Company/Product | URL | Log-in |
|  |  |  |
| Password | | | |
| & Revised | | | |
| Passwords | | | |
| Company/Product | URL | Log-in |
|  |  |  |
| Password | | | |
| & Revised | | | |
| Passwords | | | |
| Company/Product | URL | Log-in |
|  |  |  |
| Password | | | |
| & Revised | | | |
| Passwords | | | |

| Company/Product | URL | Log-in |
| --- | --- | --- |
|  |  |  |
| Password |  |  |
| & Revised |  |  |
| Passwords |  |  |

| Company/Product | URL | Log-in |
| --- | --- | --- |
|  |  |  |
| Password |  |  |
| & Revised |  |  |
| Passwords |  |  |

| Company/Product | URL | Log-in |
| --- | --- | --- |
|  |  |  |
| Password |  |  |
| & Revised |  |  |
| Passwords |  |  |

| Company/Product | URL | Log-in |
| --- | --- | --- |
|  |  |  |
| Password |  |  |
| & Revised |  |  |
| Passwords |  |  |

| Company/Product | URL | Log-in |
| --- | --- | --- |
|  |  |  |
| **Password** |  |  |  |
| **& Revised** |  |  |  |
| **Passwords** |  |  |  |
| Company/Product | URL | Log-in |
|  |  |  |
| **Password** |  |  |  |
| **& Revised** |  |  |  |
| **Passwords** |  |  |  |
| Company/Product | URL | Log-in |
|  |  |  |
| **Password** |  |  |  |
| **& Revised** |  |  |  |
| **Passwords** |  |  |  |
| Company/Product | URL | Log-in |
|  |  |  |
| **Password** |  |  |  |
| **& Revised** |  |  |  |
| **Passwords** |  |  |  |

| Company/Product | URL | Log-in |
| --- | --- | --- |
| | | |
| Password | | |
| & Revised | | |
| Passwords | | |
| Company/Product | URL | Log-in |
| | | |
| Password | | |
| & Revised | | |
| Passwords | | |
| Company/Product | URL | Log-in |
| | | |
| Password | | |
| & Revised | | |
| Passwords | | |
| Company/Product | URL | Log-in |
| | | |
| Password | | |
| & Revised | | |
| Passwords | | |

# T

| Company/Product | URL | Log-in |
| --- | --- | --- |
| | | |
| Password | | | |
| & Revised | | | |
| Passwords | | | |
| Company/Product | URL | Log-in |
| | | |
| Password | | | |
| & Revised | | | |
| Passwords | | | |
| Company/Product | URL | Log-in |
| | | |
| Password | | | |
| & Revised | | | |
| Passwords | | | |
| Company/Product | URL | Log-in |
| | | |
| Password | | | |
| & Revised | | | |
| Passwords | | | |

| Company/Product | URL | Log-in |
| --- | --- | --- |
|  |  |  |

| Password | | | |
| --- | --- | --- | --- |
| & Revised | | | |
| Passwords | | | |

| Company/Product | URL | Log-in |
| --- | --- | --- |
|  |  |  |

| Password | | | |
| --- | --- | --- | --- |
| & Revised | | | |
| Passwords | | | |

| Company/Product | URL | Log-in |
| --- | --- | --- |
|  |  |  |

| Password | | | |
| --- | --- | --- | --- |
| & Revised | | | |
| Passwords | | | |

| Company/Product | URL | Log-in |
| --- | --- | --- |
|  |  |  |

| Password | | | |
| --- | --- | --- | --- |
| & Revised | | | |
| Passwords | | | |

| Company/Product | URL | Log-in |
|---|---|---|
|  |  |  |
| **Password** |  |  |  |
| **& Revised** |  |  |  |
| **Passwords** |  |  |  |

| Company/Product | URL | Log-in |
|---|---|---|
|  |  |  |
| **Password** |  |  |  |
| **& Revised** |  |  |  |
| **Passwords** |  |  |  |

| Company/Product | URL | Log-in |
|---|---|---|
|  |  |  |
| **Password** |  |  |  |
| **& Revised** |  |  |  |
| **Passwords** |  |  |  |

| Company/Product | URL | Log-in |
|---|---|---|
|  |  |  |
| **Password** |  |  |  |
| **& Revised** |  |  |  |
| **Passwords** |  |  |  |

| Company/Product | URL | Log-in |
| --- | --- | --- |
| | | |
| Password | | | |
| & Revised | | | |
| Passwords | | | |

| Company/Product | URL | Log-in |
| --- | --- | --- |
| | | |
| Password | | | |
| & Revised | | | |
| Passwords | | | |

| Company/Product | URL | Log-in |
| --- | --- | --- |
| | | |
| Password | | | |
| & Revised | | | |
| Passwords | | | |

| Company/Product | URL | Log-in |
| --- | --- | --- |
| | | |
| Password | | | |
| & Revised | | | |
| Passwords | | | |

| Company/Product | URL | Log-in |
| --- | --- | --- |
| | | |

| Password | | | |
| --- | --- | --- | --- |
| & Revised | | | |
| Passwords | | | |

| Company/Product | URL | Log-in |
| --- | --- | --- |
| | | |

| Password | | | |
| --- | --- | --- | --- |
| & Revised | | | |
| Passwords | | | |

| Company/Product | URL | Log-in |
| --- | --- | --- |
| | | |

| Password | | | |
| --- | --- | --- | --- |
| & Revised | | | |
| Passwords | | | |

| Company/Product | URL | Log-in |
| --- | --- | --- |
| | | |

| Password | | | |
| --- | --- | --- | --- |
| & Revised | | | |
| Passwords | | | |

| Company/Product | | URL | Log-in |
| --- | --- | --- | --- |
| | | | |
| Password | | | |
| & Revised | | | |
| Passwords | | | |
| Company/Product | | URL | Log-in |
| | | | |
| Password | | | |
| & Revised | | | |
| Passwords | | | |
| Company/Product | | URL | Log-in |
| | | | |
| Password | | | |
| & Revised | | | |
| Passwords | | | |
| Company/Product | | URL | Log-in |
| | | | |
| Password | | | |
| & Revised | | | |
| Passwords | | | |

# U

| Company/Product | URL | Log-in |
| --- | --- | --- |
|  |  |  |
| Password |  |  |
| & Revised |  |  |
| Passwords |  |  |
| Company/Product | URL | Log-in |
|  |  |  |
| Password |  |  |
| & Revised |  |  |
| Passwords |  |  |
| Company/Product | URL | Log-in |
|  |  |  |
| Password |  |  |
| & Revised |  |  |
| Passwords |  |  |
| Company/Product | URL | Log-in |
|  |  |  |
| Password |  |  |
| & Revised |  |  |
| Passwords |  |  |

| Company/Product | URL | Log-in |
| --- | --- | --- |
| | | |
| Password | | | |
| & Revised | | | |
| Passwords | | | |

| Company/Product | URL | Log-in |
| --- | --- | --- |
| | | |
| Password | | | |
| & Revised | | | |
| Passwords | | | |

| Company/Product | URL | Log-in |
| --- | --- | --- |
| | | |
| Password | | | |
| & Revised | | | |
| Passwords | | | |

| Company/Product | URL | Log-in |
| --- | --- | --- |
| | | |
| Password | | | |
| & Revised | | | |
| Passwords | | | |

# V

| Company/Product | URL | Log-in |
| --- | --- | --- |
| | | |

| Password | | | |
| --- | --- | --- | --- |
| & Revised | | | |
| Passwords | | | |

| Company/Product | URL | Log-in |
| --- | --- | --- |
| | | |

| Password | | | |
| --- | --- | --- | --- |
| & Revised | | | |
| Passwords | | | |

| Company/Product | URL | Log-in |
| --- | --- | --- |
| | | |

| Password | | | |
| --- | --- | --- | --- |
| & Revised | | | |
| Passwords | | | |

| Company/Product | URL | Log-in |
| --- | --- | --- |
| | | |

| Password | | | |
| --- | --- | --- | --- |
| & Revised | | | |
| Passwords | | | |

| Company/Product | URL | Log-in |
|---|---|---|
| | | |

| Password | | | |
|---|---|---|---|
| & Revised | | | |
| Passwords | | | |

| Company/Product | URL | Log-in |
|---|---|---|
| | | |

| Password | | | |
|---|---|---|---|
| & Revised | | | |
| Passwords | | | |

| Company/Product | URL | Log-in |
|---|---|---|
| | | |

| Password | | | |
|---|---|---|---|
| & Revised | | | |
| Passwords | | | |

| Company/Product | URL | Log-in |
|---|---|---|
| | | |

| Password | | | |
|---|---|---|---|
| & Revised | | | |
| Passwords | | | |

# W

| Company/Product | URL | Log-in |
| --- | --- | --- |
|  |  |  |

| Password | | |
| --- | --- | --- |
| & Revised | | |
| Passwords | | |

| Company/Product | URL | Log-in |
| --- | --- | --- |
|  |  |  |

| Password | | |
| --- | --- | --- |
| & Revised | | |
| Passwords | | |

| Company/Product | URL | Log-in |
| --- | --- | --- |
|  |  |  |

| Password | | |
| --- | --- | --- |
| & Revised | | |
| Passwords | | |

| Company/Product | URL | Log-in |
| --- | --- | --- |
|  |  |  |

| Password | | |
| --- | --- | --- |
| & Revised | | |
| Passwords | | |

| Company/Product | URL | Log-in |
|---|---|---|
|  |  |  |

| Password | | | |
|---|---|---|---|
| & Revised | | | |
| Passwords | | | |

| Company/Product | URL | Log-in |
|---|---|---|
|  |  |  |

| Password | | | |
|---|---|---|---|
| & Revised | | | |
| Passwords | | | |

| Company/Product | URL | Log-in |
|---|---|---|
|  |  |  |

| Password | | | |
|---|---|---|---|
| & Revised | | | |
| Passwords | | | |

| Company/Product | URL | Log-in |
|---|---|---|
|  |  |  |

| Password | | | |
|---|---|---|---|
| & Revised | | | |
| Passwords | | | |

| Company/Product | URL | Log-in |
| --- | --- | --- |
|  |  |  |
| Password |  |  |  |
| & Revised |  |  |  |
| Passwords |  |  |  |
| Company/Product | URL | Log-in |
|  |  |  |
| Password |  |  |  |
| & Revised |  |  |  |
| Passwords |  |  |  |
| Company/Product | URL | Log-in |
|  |  |  |
| Password |  |  |  |
| & Revised |  |  |  |
| Passwords |  |  |  |
| Company/Product | URL | Log-in |
|  |  |  |
| Password |  |  |  |
| & Revised |  |  |  |
| Passwords |  |  |  |

| Company/Product | URL | Log-in |
| --- | --- | --- |
|  |  |  |
| Password & Revised Passwords |  |  |
| Company/Product | URL | Log-in |
|  |  |  |
| Password & Revised Passwords |  |  |
| Company/Product | URL | Log-in |
|  |  |  |
| Password & Revised Passwords |  |  |
| Company/Product | URL | Log-in |
|  |  |  |
| Password & Revised Passwords |  |  |

# X

| Company/Product | URL | Log-in |
| --- | --- | --- |
|  |  |  |
| Password | | |
| & Revised | | |
| Passwords | | |
| Company/Product | URL | Log-in |
|  |  |  |
| Password | | |
| & Revised | | |
| Passwords | | |
| Company/Product | URL | Log-in |
|  |  |  |
| Password | | |
| & Revised | | |
| Passwords | | |
| Company/Product | URL | Log-in |
|  |  |  |
| Password | | |
| & Revised | | |
| Passwords | | |

| Company/Product | URL | Log-in |
| --- | --- | --- |
|  |  |  |

| Password | | | |
| --- | --- | --- | --- |
| & Revised | | | |
| Passwords | | | |

| Company/Product | URL | Log-in |
| --- | --- | --- |
|  |  |  |

| Password | | | |
| --- | --- | --- | --- |
| & Revised | | | |
| Passwords | | | |

| Company/Product | URL | Log-in |
| --- | --- | --- |
|  |  |  |

| Password | | | |
| --- | --- | --- | --- |
| & Revised | | | |
| Passwords | | | |

| Company/Product | URL | Log-in |
| --- | --- | --- |
|  |  |  |

| Password | | | |
| --- | --- | --- | --- |
| & Revised | | | |
| Passwords | | | |

# Y

| Company/Product | URL | Log-in |
|---|---|---|
|  |  |  |

| Password |  |  |  |
|---|---|---|---|
| & Revised |  |  |  |
| Passwords |  |  |  |

| Company/Product | URL | Log-in |
|---|---|---|
|  |  |  |

| Password |  |  |  |
|---|---|---|---|
| & Revised |  |  |  |
| Passwords |  |  |  |

| Company/Product | URL | Log-in |
|---|---|---|
|  |  |  |

| Password |  |  |  |
|---|---|---|---|
| & Revised |  |  |  |
| Passwords |  |  |  |

| Company/Product | URL | Log-in |
|---|---|---|
|  |  |  |

| Password |  |  |  |
|---|---|---|---|
| & Revised |  |  |  |
| Passwords |  |  |  |

| Company/Product | URL | Log-in |
| --- | --- | --- |
| | | |
| Password | | | |
| & Revised | | | |
| Passwords | | | |

| Company/Product | URL | Log-in |
| --- | --- | --- |
| | | |
| Password | | | |
| & Revised | | | |
| Passwords | | | |

| Company/Product | URL | Log-in |
| --- | --- | --- |
| | | |
| Password | | | |
| & Revised | | | |
| Passwords | | | |

| Company/Product | URL | Log-in |
| --- | --- | --- |
| | | |
| Password | | | |
| & Revised | | | |
| Passwords | | | |

# Z

| Company/Product | URL | Log-in |
| --- | --- | --- |
| | | |
| Password | | | |
| & Revised | | | |
| Passwords | | | |

| Company/Product | URL | Log-in |
| --- | --- | --- |
| | | |
| Password | | | |
| & Revised | | | |
| Passwords | | | |

| Company/Product | URL | Log-in |
| --- | --- | --- |
| | | |
| Password | | | |
| & Revised | | | |
| Passwords | | | |

| Company/Product | URL | Log-in |
| --- | --- | --- |
| | | |
| Password | | | |
| & Revised | | | |
| Passwords | | | |

| Company/Product | | URL | Log-in |
| --- | --- | --- | --- |
| | | | |
| Password | | | |
| & Revised | | | |
| Passwords | | | |
| Company/Product | | URL | Log-in |
| | | | |
| Password | | | |
| & Revised | | | |
| Passwords | | | |
| Company/Product | | URL | Log-in |
| | | | |
| Password | | | |
| & Revised | | | |
| Passwords | | | |
| Company/Product | | URL | Log-in |
| | | | |
| Password | | | |
| & Revised | | | |
| Passwords | | | |

# Other

| Company/Product | URL | Log-in |
| --- | --- | --- |
| | | |

| Password | | | |
| --- | --- | --- | --- |
| & Revised | | | |
| Passwords | | | |

| Company/Product | URL | Log-in |
| --- | --- | --- |
| | | |

| Password | | | |
| --- | --- | --- | --- |
| & Revised | | | |
| Passwords | | | |

| Company/Product | URL | Log-in |
| --- | --- | --- |
| | | |

| Password | | | |
| --- | --- | --- | --- |
| & Revised | | | |
| Passwords | | | |

| Company/Product | URL | Log-in |
| --- | --- | --- |
| | | |

| Password | | | |
| --- | --- | --- | --- |
| & Revised | | | |
| Passwords | | | |

| Company/Product | URL | Log-in |
|---|---|---|
|  |  |  |

| Password |  |  |  |
|---|---|---|---|
| & Revised |  |  |  |
| Passwords |  |  |  |

| Company/Product | URL | Log-in |
|---|---|---|
|  |  |  |

| Password |  |  |  |
|---|---|---|---|
| & Revised |  |  |  |
| Passwords |  |  |  |

| Company/Product | URL | Log-in |
|---|---|---|
|  |  |  |

| Password |  |  |  |
|---|---|---|---|
| & Revised |  |  |  |
| Passwords |  |  |  |

| Company/Product | URL | Log-in |
|---|---|---|
|  |  |  |

| Password |  |  |  |
|---|---|---|---|
| & Revised |  |  |  |
| Passwords |  |  |  |

| Company/Product | | URL | | Log-in | |
|---|---|---|---|---|---|
| | | | | | |
| Password | | | | | |
| & Revised | | | | | |
| Passwords | | | | | |
| Company/Product | | URL | | Log-in | |
| | | | | | |
| Password | | | | | |
| & Revised | | | | | |
| Passwords | | | | | |
| Company/Product | | URL | | Log-in | |
| | | | | | |
| Password | | | | | |
| & Revised | | | | | |
| Passwords | | | | | |
| Company/Product | | URL | | Log-in | |
| | | | | | |
| Password | | | | | |
| & Revised | | | | | |
| Passwords | | | | | |

| Company/Product | URL | Log-in |
|---|---|---|
| | | |

| | | | |
|---|---|---|---|
| Password | | | |
| & Revised | | | |
| Passwords | | | |

| Company/Product | URL | Log-in |
|---|---|---|
| | | |

| | | | |
|---|---|---|---|
| Password | | | |
| & Revised | | | |
| Passwords | | | |

| Company/Product | URL | Log-in |
|---|---|---|
| | | |

| | | | |
|---|---|---|---|
| Password | | | |
| & Revised | | | |
| Passwords | | | |

| Company/Product | URL | Log-in |
|---|---|---|
| | | |

| | | | |
|---|---|---|---|
| Password | | | |
| & Revised | | | |
| Passwords | | | |

| Company/Product | URL | Log-in |
| --- | --- | --- |
| | | |
| **Password** | | |
| **& Revised** | | |
| **Passwords** | | |
| Company/Product | URL | Log-in |
| | | |
| **Password** | | |
| **& Revised** | | |
| **Passwords** | | |
| Company/Product | URL | Log-in |
| | | |
| **Password** | | |
| **& Revised** | | |
| **Passwords** | | |
| Company/Product | URL | Log-in |
| | | |
| **Password** | | |
| **& Revised** | | |
| **Passwords** | | |

| Company/Product | URL | Log-in |
| --- | --- | --- |
|  |  |  |
| **Password** |  |  |  |
| **& Revised** |  |  |  |
| **Passwords** |  |  |  |

| Company/Product | URL | Log-in |
| --- | --- | --- |
|  |  |  |
| **Password** |  |  |  |
| **& Revised** |  |  |  |
| **Passwords** |  |  |  |

| Company/Product | URL | Log-in |
| --- | --- | --- |
|  |  |  |
| **Password** |  |  |  |
| **& Revised** |  |  |  |
| **Passwords** |  |  |  |

| Company/Product | URL | Log-in |
| --- | --- | --- |
|  |  |  |
| **Password** |  |  |  |
| **& Revised** |  |  |  |
| **Passwords** |  |  |  |

# **About the Author**

Linda Fostek is an International Speaker, Author and Consultant on a mission to empower others to get off the Worry-go-round and become their own *Master of Disaster.*

Linda knows first-hand how preparation and planning allows companies and individuals to navigate through and thrive when blindsided by life.

She is constantly seeking solutions to improve the lives of others.  Her mission to reduce worry about the "What ifs" of life by avoiding family conflicts, recovering from disaster quicker, and reducing the chaos of life is part of everything she does.

As The Crisis Planner, Linda brings her expertise, creative solutions, kind heart and compassion together guiding others through planning for the inevitable life and business challenges. Inspired by her late father, Norbert Osiecki, Linda, carries on his legacy through her recent books *And Now What?* and *Shit Happens.*

Her passion for networking resulted in the release of her Amazon best-selling book *Love/Hate Networking.*  Linda was named 2017 Networker of the year by 516/631 Ads a prominent Long Island Networking resource.  She was recently profiled in The Long Island Business News Who's Who 2018 Business Services and Honored as a 2018 NY Power Woman.

Linda is the co-leader of the Nassau and Suffolk chapters of Women's Prosperity Network an international organization that inspires women to unleash the greatness that lies within.  She is a Certified Speaker, member of *The One Philosophy* Founders Circle, part of the Awakening Giants mission for global transformation, Board Member of Long Island National Aging in Place Council, Member of PULSE Center for Patient Safety Education & Advocacy, Certified Trainer for MedXPrime, member of Orion Resource Group and The Association of Continency Professionals.

Linda has appeared on "Live It Up" with Donna Drake, "Tai and the Music Man" on WLINY, "Passion for Life with Dee and Friends" on Madhouse TV, "Happy Sunday Morning" with David Gussin and "The Caregivers Caregiver" with David Nassaney.

# For more information on

**Booking Linda to Speak
at your next event
and/or
The Crisis Planner
Products and Services
Book Sales
Customized Books
Bulk Purchases**

## Contact us at:

**TheCrisisPlanner.com
LindaFostek@TheCrisisPlanner.com
631-3685005**

## Check this out!

## Introducing

## The Crisis Planner HOME System

Your complete
Home Operation Manual and Emergency System
Keep you and your family safe and secure
no matter what life hands you.

www.ingramcontent.com/pod-product-compliance
Lightning Source LLC
Chambersburg PA
CBHW070133260726
48658CB00001B/394